My Mommy's Not Happy Anymore:

A Children's Book To Help Kids Understand Postpartum Depression

by: Britt LeBoeuf

Copyright © 2019 Britt LeBoeuf

All rights reserved. This book or any portion thereof may not be reproduced or used in any manner whatsoever without the express written permission of the publisher except for the use of brief quotations in a book review.

Published by Amazon Kindle Direct Publishing

Interior artwork TopVectors via Vectorstock.com

Cover art by TopVectors and Canva.com

Author contact: brittboeuf@yahoo.com

ISBN: 9781981853656

This is a work of fiction. Names, characters, businesses, places, events and incidents are either the products of the author's imagination or used in a fictitious manner. Any resemblance to actual persons, living or dead, or actual events is purely coincidental.

For all the mothers that have suffered from Postpartum Depression and Anxiety and their sweet babes, including my own loving mother Bridget and my beloved children Liam and Cullen.

Hi! My name is Luke! I'm 5 years old.

I like playing with trucks, petting my dog Scout and spending time with my mom and dad.

My parents and I have so much fun together!

We play, sing, dance and read books.

One day at dinner, my parents told me that my mom had a baby in her belly and that I was going to be a big brother.

I was so excited! I had always wanted a sibling!

Mommy's belly started to get bigger.

She told me that her belly was getting bigger because my new little brother or sister was growing inside of it and that before too long, he or she would be on the outside of her belly instead of on the inside.

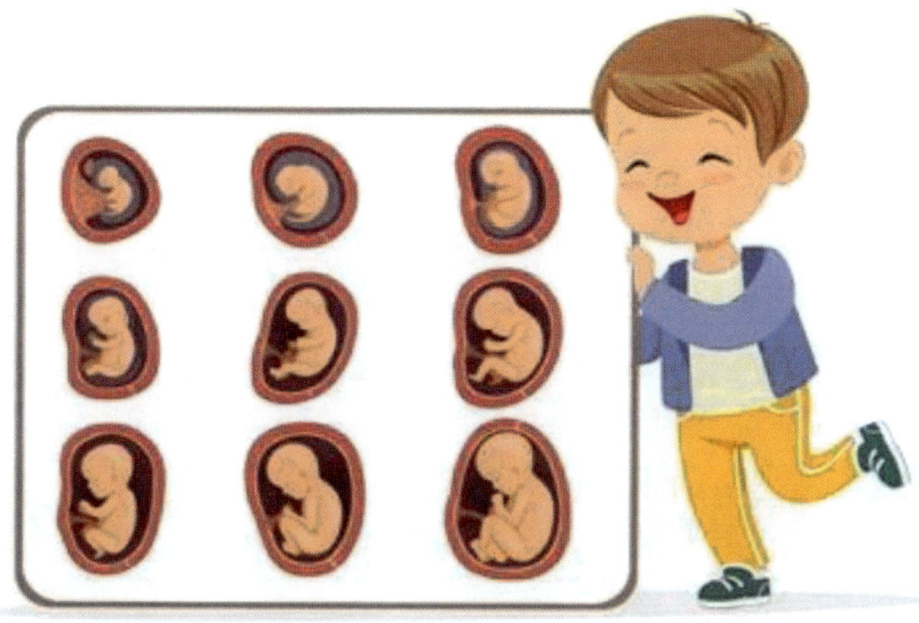

As the baby grew in mommy's belly, she showed me what it looked like as time went by.

It started out very tiny and kept getting bigger every week.

One day mommy and daddy came home from a doctor's appointment and told me that the doctor said the baby was a boy.

I was going to have a new little brother!

Until one day, Daddy had to take Mommy to the hospital so she could have my new little brother.

Grandma came to stay with me and Scout.

Mom and Dad returned home from the hospital a few days later with my new baby brother, Sam.

I'm having so much fun with my new little brother. He is so tiny and sleeps a lot.

But, I really like helping mom and dad take care of him.

My little brother cries a lot. He wakes me up sometimes at night too.

Mom and I take naps in the living room sometimes during the day while dad takes care of Sam.

Dad is going back to work today.

Scout and I are going to stay home and help mom with the house chores and the baby.

After dad left, Sam went in his room for a nap. Mom let me play with her tablet for a while.

I was so excited! She had never let me use her tablet before!

I was being too loud and accidentally woke Sam up from his nap. Mom got mad at me.

She yelled at me and told me to go to my room for waking my brother up. I didn't mean to wake him up!

Daddy took Sam and me to the park today.
Dad said Mommy needs a day to herself so it'll be just us boys today.

Daddy and I are doing some chores around the house while Mommy and Sam take a nap.

Daddy said helping out right now is really important for our family.

Mommy and Daddy were talking in the living room.

Mommy looked really sad. I'm not sure what they were talking about, but I'm really worried about my mommy.

Grandma came over to pick up Sam and I to go for a sleepover at her house. I will miss mommy and daddy, but I'm really excited to go over to Grandma's house with my brother.

I wanted to say goodbye to Mommy before we left for Grandma's, but Daddy said she was tired and was taking a nap.

When we were at Grandma's house, Grandma and I played while Sam took his nap.

It was fun to play with Grandma, but I was also really worried about Mommy and missed her a lot.

The next day, Grandma brought Sam and me home.

When we got there, Mommy gave me a big hug. She told me that she was sorry that she had been so sad and mean lately, but that it was because she had something called Postpartum Depression.

Mommy told me that she went to see her doctor while we were at Grandma's. Her doctor helped Mommy figure out why she had been sad.

The doctor said Postpartum Depression can happen sometimes after mommies have babies and it can be scary, but that with her help, Mommy would start to feel better.

Mommy kept going to see her doctor to get help with her Postpartum Depression.

Now, she is feeling a lot better and seems much happier than she was before.

Sam is getting bigger. He smiles a lot more and cries a lot less. I can't wait until he starts walking and we can run and play together.

Mommy is feeling all better now too!

I love having my happy mommy back again. I am glad that she got help from her doctor for her Postpartum Depression.

I feel bad that she had to go through that, but I sure am glad that we can do stuff together again and now my little brother can join too.

Made in the USA
Las Vegas, NV
02 October 2024